Stop Swinging on your Chair

Samantha Fawkes

Presentation by *BookLeaf Publishing*

Web: www.bookleafpub.com

E-mail: info@bookleafpub.com

ISBN: 9789357740463

First edition 2022

DEDICATION

I dedicate this book to all of the fantastic young people who have sat in my classroom and given me a story to tell.

ACKNOWLEDGEMENT

Thank you to all who have inspired me, encouraged me and supported me to get to the point of my life where I am willing to take a risk such as this.

PREFACE

Hopefully these poems will make you laugh, make you think and maybe you appreciate what those of us who teach do day in day out because we care. Care has been taken to ensure most of these poems are comical in their own right but based on true stories.

Monday Morning

Pulling up in the car park,
winter morning's are dark.
I feel like I should still be sleeping,
even though the birds are cheeping.

Inside my classroom I drop,
my bags, my books and stop.
I need to get to the printer,
It's time to become a sprinter.

A queue already, it's only seven!
I think to myself good heavens!
What's that? A beeping sound?
Twist the waster toner round!

Of course the printer is broken,
the next teacher says you must be jokin'.
I wish I was, I stand and shake my head,
Oh how I wish I was still in bed!

Someone turns up with a magic touch,
they say it didn't take much.
I thank them with a gracious heart,
I print my sheets and off I dart!

The Art Lesson

Today we are going to paint some flowers,
that was what I told the class.
The minutes felt like hours,
clean tables were sparse.

Red, yellow, orange, green and blue,
why is Beth's hair pink?
My oh my, what will I do?
what will her mother think?

A cup of water spills on the table,
paint brushes are used as swords.
I do wish the young ones were more able,
and there wasn't paint on my cords!

Let's put your pictures up to dry,
and clean the tables so they shine!
A successful lesson besides the hair dye,
it's lunch time now, form a line.

Don't Swing On Your Chair!

I've told them all the story many times before,
yet here is little Aron swinging to and fro.
The little boy many years ago, swung so hard,
he fell and cracked his head open!

Aron says, that's not true miss, no way!
I'm never going to stop swinging!
Four on the floor I say and watch,
he puts two feet on the ground and smirks.

I shake my head and say, well I warned you!
We carry on learning our times tables.
Aron is swinging, faster and faster,
further back with each swing...

C - R - A - S - H
Aron! I shout, are you okay?
The rest of the class laughing..
Aron gets up from the floor,
I guess I should stop swinging he says.

Sports Day Games

A game of balance and speed,
boiled or not?
A spoon is needed,
and great concentration.

Choose a partner,
tie a leg each, together.
Arms around each other,
keep in time and run for your life!

Spaced out around the track,
who is the fastest?
The whistle blows and they're off,
cross the line!

Hold it behind your head,
look straight ahead,
Extend your arm,
and throw it ahead!

Aim for the target,
stand side on.
Pull your arm back,
and release!

A little run up,
getting ready to jump.
There's the line,
now fly into the pit!

What Am I?

1.

I join things together.
I often lose my lid.
I can dry easily.
My shape is a cylinder.

2.

I'm full of lots of horizontal lines.
I have one vertical line.
I open.
I close.

3.

Children tidy up quickly for this.
I'm fun.
I seem to be over too quickly.
There are only normally two a day.

4.

I am very important.
Without me no work gets completed.
I start off long.
I get shorter as the days go by.

5.
I get left out.
Every child has one.
I hurt teacher's feet.
Children like to swing on me.

Teachers Moving Classrooms

The end of the year is here,
I'm moving classroom.
My new room is bigger, I cheer,
but moving fills me with doom.

When did I acquire so many books?
When did I last open this drawer?
Are these all my jackets on these hooks?
I spread everything out over the floor.

This needs to go to the new year two class!
Oh this is mine, for my room upstairs.
My TA stands by and takes things I pass,
In a corner, a pile of teddy bears!

So far, eight shopping bags are full,
bursting at the brim, ready to go.
I need to check behind that unit, I pull,
ARGHHH a spider, oh no, no!

Behind the unit, there are:
13 pens, a story book and a memo.

I knew that book couldn't have got far!
In the bags, these things I stow.

A whole day later I think I'm ready to move,
up and down the stairs again and again.
The heaviest bag, my strength I'll prove!
My arm hurts, but, no pain no gain.

I step in the door when the handle snaps!
Piles of stickers, pens, papers and more!
My TA stands, grinning and claps,
I kneel down and pile up the things from the
floor.

Once everything is in its place,
a great big smile across my face.
It's time for something new,
where shall I start? What shall I do?

A School Day

It's 6am my alarm is ringing,
a new day, is just beginning.
I get up and get ready for my day,
I wonder what will come my way?

I get to school I need to print,
no queue I have to sprint!
I place the paper in the drawer,
and think to myself, score!

The the beeping starts, and error code,
how can I get it out of this mode?
I try and find the paper that is jammed,
no sign, I shut the doors, no I slammed!

Along comes another teacher, help I cry!
they fix it in an instant, in a blink of an eye!
I thank them over and over,
they must be my four-leafed clover!

Back to class, the children start to come in,
hello and good morning I stand and grin.
Tommy has a face like thunder,
what's wrong I wonder!

Tommy tells me he's been in trouble,
for popping his little sister's bubble.
She started it by blowing them in his face,
so he squished it, gone without a trace.

I tell him it's okay to worry,
but I'm sure it'll be over in a hurry.
He gives me a little smile,
and talks to his friend about the daily mile.

After the register it's time for reading,
look back a the page I'm pleading!
Claire, can you read with the book upside down?
She turns it round and gives me a frown.

Now it's time for maths, whiteboards out,
whiteboards and pens out, I shout!
Try this one, hold up your boards,
points are given as rewards!

Finally break time is here,
hooray the children cheer.
Tidy your things as quick as you can,
after play we'll do our writing plan.

Outside it's the calm before the storm,
fights in football are the norm.
Children swing from the monkey bars,
others talking about who created stars?

Line up we shout, no issues today,
like I said that's not a normal day.
Back to class, sat facing the front,
to plan our argument, we must be blunt.

The children get on working well,
until someone comes to tell.
Misssss, he took my pencil from me!
You have a pencil in your hand I see?

Yes, but it's not my pencil miss,
I knew it wouldn't last, this bliss.
Give her the pencil back I command,
he places it in her hand.

Thank you, now can we get on?
I've finished someone yells, I've won!
It's not a race, I reply, check you work,
already have miss, they smirk.

I go over and check it and what do I find?
no capital letters or full stops I remind.
Read your sentences through again and again,
any mistakes, one line through with your pen.

Finally it's time for lunch, line up at the door,
and try not to drop your food on the floor!
Have a nice lunch time and be kind,

any problems, it's your supervisor you find!

In the afternoon, it's PE,
the children shout yipee.
Getting changed takes what seems like hours,
lets try and develop some changing
superpowers!

The end of the day comes upon us,
let's get ready, please no fuss...
I open the door to a see of faces,
luckily parents stand in the same places!

I am

I am:
A parent
A nurse
A dentist
A wrestling referee
A hairdresser
A cleaner
A comedian
A storyteller
A musician
A fitness coach
An artist
An organiser
I am, a teacher.

The Paper Towel

Who knew that schools have a magical towel?
It sits by the sink waiting for its moment.
The moment a grazed knee or scraped arm
comes.
Eagerly it waits to be picked up.
It flies in a hand towards the running tap.
SPLOSH!
The water smothers the towel.
Next is gently floats down towards a sea of red.
A muffled crying starts to slow.
A few moments later its job is done.

Lunchtime

What is it with lunchtime?
My angelic class suddenly transform.
Into a herd of charging elephants,
frantically making their way to the hall.

Don't run, my pleading fails to stop them!
They will not stop now, crashing through the
doors.
Sandwiches plonk themselves down and dinner
line up.
Conversations at a deafening volume fill the
hall.

Within minutes, the food has been inhaled.
Miss can we go out now? Miss? Miss?
Just a moment, wait until more children are
ready.
Then. The. Doors. Open.

A great cheer and a rush to the door take place,
the children sprint outside and soak up the
outdoors.
Then danger strikes... a football!
I thought we hid that ball? I think to myself.

No sooner after the football was spotted is the
first foul.
He kicked me! Miss he kicked me!
No miss, it was a tackle, just an accident.
Right, stop fighting or there'll be no more
football!

A Teacher's Secret

A teacher secret,
remember to turn around,
when you want to smirk!

Summer Holidays

Stopping all the morning alarms
Unwinding to the max!
Meeting up with family and friends
Making lots of plans
Evenings out for dinner
Remembering life is fun!

Happy memories being made
Optician appointments
Lazy days
Ironing put on hold
Day trips exploring
A day of binge watching TV
Yummy food being cooked
Sadness when they're over!

My First Year of Teaching

I stood at the front and started to shake,
can I change my mind or is it too late?
To trust me to be in charge of a class,
you've got to be having a laugh?

No teacher presence, no routines,
what a nightmare, I thought it'd be a dream.
Should that child be doing that?
I'll ask my TA, he seems a nice chap!

I remember the day a kid stole my shoe,
I really just didn't know what to do.
He sat on it laughing out loud,
I've never seen a face so proud!

The first class I had, I will always hold dear,
the memories we have will forever be near.
The first school trip to the safari park,
the end of the year when I didn't want to part!

Singing Assembly

Some of the songs we sing,
really make my ears ring.
So out of tune, so slow,
those songs really need to go!

When the children sing super high,
sitting up straight, reaching the sky.
Who is the child singing in a silly way?
and look they think it's time to play!

Clapping out of time,
not listening for the chime.
The singing seems to increase in speed,
the teacher at the front taking the lead.

Have we got time for one more?
Oh, Miss is opening the door.
We'll sing this on the way out,
remember, sing, don't shout!

You're my Favourite

Children always say,
you're their favourite teacher,
and then they move on.

The Best Thing About Teaching

The best thing about teaching,
isn't the data or progress.
It isn't being told you've done a good job,
or parents thanking you.
It isn't meeting targets or having no marking,
the holidays are good but ti's not that!

It's those light bulb moments,
or when the whole class erupts in laughter.
It's the children being enthusiastic about their
learning,
and sharing their ideas with the class!
It's knowing you made a child smile today,
and feeling proud of the children!

Seeing a Child at the Supermarket

There's Tommy with his Mum and Dad,
he's been told off, he looks sad.
I turn down an aisle out of sight,
Why did I have to pop in tonight.

In my trolley goes milk and cheese,
I hear Tommy say he thinks he will freeze.
Oh no, they're getting closer to me,
I just popped in to get something for tea!

I make it to the bread aisle and pick up some
rolls,
when around the corner Tommy strolls.
I try not to make any eye contact,
how I wish the store was packed!

All of a sudden I hear...
Hi miss in my ear!
Hello, I manage to smile,
then awkwardly chat for a while.

I speed off to pay for my things,
the scanner constantly dings.
Oh no I say out loud to myself,
nothing for tea from the shelf!

The Missing Pencil

Miss, I've lost my pencil.
What do you mean you've lost your pencil?
I can't find it miss.
Did you have it last lesson?
Yes, but I don't have it now.
Miss sighs and raises her brow.

The rest of the table start looking,
books are lifted and chairs are shifted.
It's not under here, or behind here!
How can it just vanish they cry?
This is a waste of your time,
and just then we hear the bell chime.

The School Trip

Seated, belted, the driver turns the key,
Out of the window what ca you see?
10 minutes in, Miss you need to help Nick,
he thinks he's going to be sick!

A sick bag is given to him,
I hope he doesn't, it'll be grim!
He starts to feel better - hooray!
Maybe this won't be such a bad day!

After an hour we arrive at the zoo,
Miss, Miss what are we going to do?
Let's hang on a minute and check the map,
It's very sunny, so put on your cap.

First up, the playful emperor penguins,
watching them fills the children with grins.
After that the reptile house, with the snakes,
I hear a boy say he hopes he has two cakes!

When we get to the meerkats I laugh,
a child asked if it was a baby giraffe!
The tigers prowl up and down, all around,
ready to pounce, standing their ground.

Then it's time to have some lunch,
all that can be heard is crunch, crunch, crunch.
The children start to finish eating,
We talk about the time we will be meeting.

Another walk all around the zoo,
counting the children...22!
No one has been lost or left behind,
that's a weight off my mind!

The bus home is silent, apart from some snoring,
well at least no one can say the ride was boring!
Slowing to a stop, we're back at school,
then we hear: "man that was cool!"

Planning a Lesson

Here is my idea,
now lets change it twenty times,
and use the first one!

The Year is Over

The end of the year is happy and sad,
but overall I feel glad.
The children are ready to move on,
I feel like I've won.

They year flies by so fast,
but we really have had a blast!
I hope the children had a good year,
the memories, I'll hold dear.

The laughter and the fun,
always saying well done!
They all made me smile,
nearly all the while!

I will miss my class,
but in the corridors we shall pass.
I wish them all the best,
it feels like they're leaving the nest!